ANIMAL FEET
A Song about Animal Adaptations

By VITA JIMÉNEZ
Illustrations by KATY HUDSON
Music by DREW TEMPERANTE

CANTATA
LEARNING

WWW.CANTATALEARNING.COM

CANTATA
LEARNING

Published by Cantata Learning
1710 Roe Crest Drive
North Mankato, MN 56003
www.cantatalearning.com

A note to educators and librarians from the publisher: Cantata Learning has provided the following data to assist in book processing and suggested use of Cantata Learning product.

Publisher's Cataloging-in-Publication Data
Prepared by Librarian Consultant: Ann-Marie Begnaud
Library of Congress Control Number: 2016937884
    Animal Feet : A Song about Animal Adaptations
    Series: Animal World : Songs about Animal Adaptations
    By Vita Jiménez
    Illustrations by Katy Hudson
    Music by Drew Temperante
    Summary: Full-color illustrations and music help readers discover how animals have adapted their feet for different uses.
    ISBN: 978-1-63290-763-9 (library binding/CD)
Suggested Dewey and Subject Headings:
    Dewey: E 591.4
    LCSH Subject Headings: Animals – Adaptation – Juvenile literature. | Foot – Anatomy – Juvenile literature. | Animals – Adaptation – Songs and Music – Texts. | Foot – Anatomy – Songs and Music – Texts. | Animals – Adaptation – Juvenile sound recordings. | Foot – Anatomy – Juvenile sound recordings.
    Sears Subject Headings: Adaptation (Biology). | Animals – Anatomy. | Foot. | School songbooks. | Children's songs. |
    BISAC Subject Headings: JUVENILE NONFICTION / Science & Nature / Anatomy & Physiology. | JUVENILE NONFICTION / Music / Songbooks. | JUVENILE NONFICTION / Animals / General.

Book design and art direction: Tim Palin Creative
Editorial direction: Flat Sole Studio
Music direction: Elizabeth Draper
Music written and produced by Drew Temperante

Printed in the United States of America in North Mankato, Minnesota.
122016   0339CGS17

ACCESS THE MUSIC!

SCAN CODE WITH MOBILE APP

CANTATALEARNING.COM

TIPS TO SUPPORT LITERACY AT HOME

WHY READING AND SINGING WITH YOUR CHILD IS SO IMPORTANT

Daily reading with your child leads to increased academic achievement. Music and songs, specifically rhyming songs, are a fun and easy way to build early literacy and language development. Music skills correlate significantly with both phonological awareness and reading development. Singing helps build vocabulary and speech development. And reading and appreciating music together is a wonderful way to strengthen your relationship.

READ AND SING EVERY DAY!

TIPS FOR USING CANTATA LEARNING BOOKS AND SONGS DURING YOUR DAILY STORY TIME

1. As you sing and read, point out the different words on the page that rhyme. Suggest other words that rhyme.

2. Memorize simple rhymes such as Itsy Bitsy Spider and sing them together. This encourages comprehension skills and early literacy skills.

3. Use the questions in the back of each book to guide your singing and storytelling.

4. Read the included sheet music with your child while you listen to the song. How do the music notes correlate to the words of the song?

5. Sing along on the go and at home. Access music by scanning the QR code on each Cantata book, or by using the included CD. You can also stream or download the music for free to your computer, smartphone, or mobile device.

Devoting time to daily reading shows that you are available for your child. Together, you are building language, literacy, and listening skills.

Have fun reading and singing!

Animal feet come in many shapes and sizes. Some animals have claws or hooves on their feet. Others have webbed feet or sticky toes. Many animals use their feet to do more than just walk or run. Some use their feet to **paddle**, dig, and even taste!

To find out more about animals and their amazing feet, turn the page and sing along!

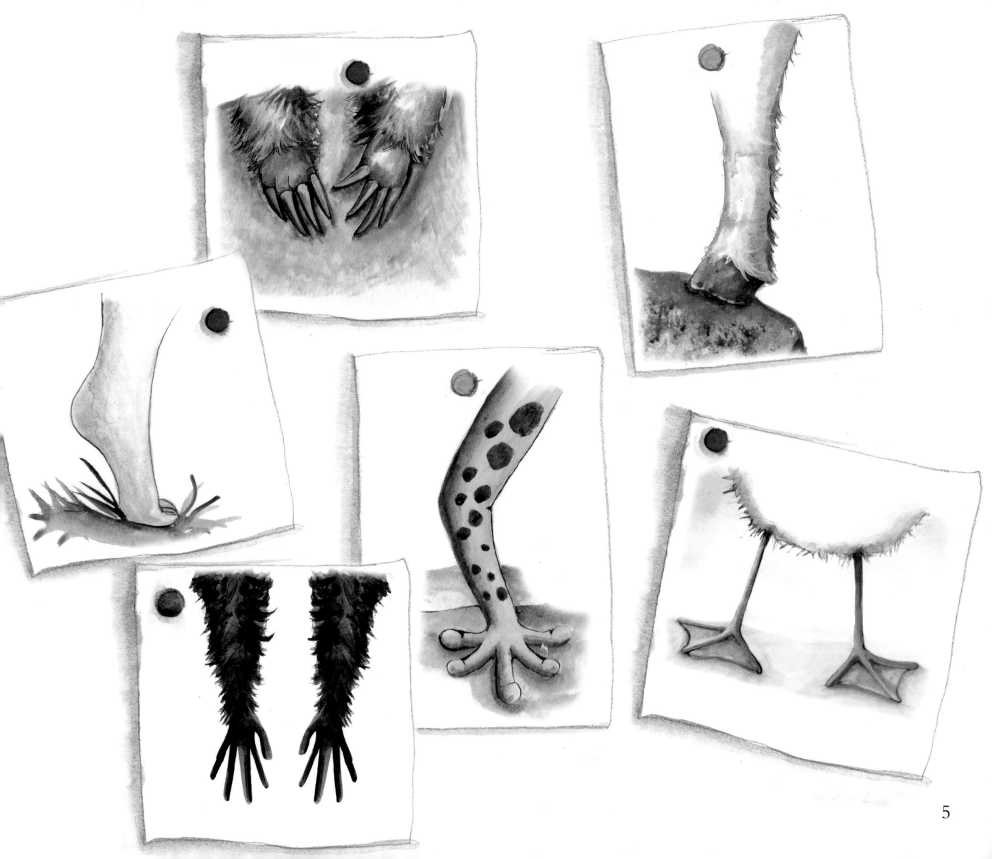

5

What can **gophers** do with their feet?

They run and dig, dig, dig.
Gopher feet just can't be **beat**!

What can gorillas do with their feet?

They climb and eat, eat, eat.
Gorilla feet just can't be beat!

9

What can **geckos** do with their feet?

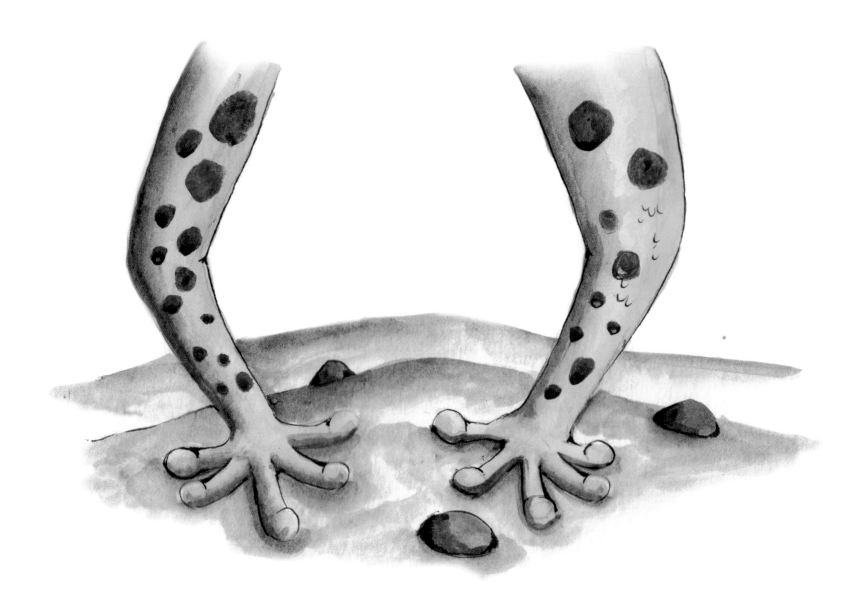

They **cling** and stick, stick, stick.
Gecko feet just can't be beat!

What can bats do with their feet?

They grab and hang, hang, hang.
Bat feet just can't be beat!

13

What can ducks do with their feet?

They swim and paddle, paddle, paddle.
Duck feet just can't be beat!

What can butterflies do with their feet?

They stand and taste, taste, taste.
Butterfly feet just can't be beat!

What can mountain goats do with their feet?

They run and jump, jump, jump.
Mountain goat feet just can't be beat!

What can people do with their feet?

They can walk, run, swim, dance, kick, jump, and **leap**!
Their feet just can't be beat!

SONG LYRICS
Animal Feet

What can gophers do with their feet?
They run and dig, dig, dig.
Gopher feet just can't be beat!

What can gorillas do with their feet?
They climb and eat, eat, eat.
Gorilla feet just can't be beat!

What can geckos do with their feet?
They cling and stick, stick, stick.
Gecko feet just can't be beat!

What can bats do with their feet?
They grab and hang, hang, hang.
Bat feet just can't be beat!

What can ducks do with their feet?
They swim and paddle, paddle, paddle.
Duck feet just can't be beat!

What can butterflies do with their feet?
They stand and taste, taste, taste.
Butterfly feet just can't be beat!

What can mountain goats do with
   their feet?
They run and jump, jump, jump.
Mountain goat feet just can't be beat!

What can people do with their feet?
They can walk, run, swim, dance, kick,
   jump, and leap!
Their feet just can't be beat!

Animal Feet

Hip Hop
Drew Temperante

Verse

1. What can go-phers do with their feet? They run and dig, dig, dig.

Go-pher feet just can't be beat!

Verse 2
What can gorillas do with their feet?
They climb and eat, eat, eat.
Gorilla feet just can't be beat!

Verse 3
What can geckos do with their feet?
They cling and stick, stick, stick.
Gecko feet just can't be beat!

Verse 4
What can bats do with their feet?
They grab and hang, hang, hang.
Bat feet just can't be beat!

Verse 5
What can ducks do with their feet?
They swim and paddle, paddle, paddle.
Duck feet just can't be beat!

Verse 6
What can butterflies do with their feet?
They stand and taste, taste, taste.
Butterfly feet just can't be beat!

Verse 7
What can mountain goats do with their feet?
They run and jump, jump, jump.
Mountain goat feet just can't be beat!

Verse 8

8. What can peo-ple do with their feet? They can walk, run, swim, dance, kick, jump, and leap!

Their feet just can't be beat!

GLOSSARY

beat—be better than

gecko—a small lizard

gopher—a small, furry animal that lives underground

leap—jump

paddle—use feet to move through the water

GUIDED READING ACTIVITIES

1. This song talks about the ways animals use their feet. Are there other ways animals use their feet that were not mentioned in the song?

2. Look back at the pictures in this book. How do they help you understand the text?

3. Draw a picture of your foot. Then draw the foot of an animal listed in this book. How are your feet different? How are they the same?

TO LEARN MORE

Hulbert, Laura. *Who Has These Feet?* New York: Henry Holt and Co., 2011.

Markle, Sandra. *What If You Had Animal Feet?* New York: Scholastic, 2015.

Royston, Angela. *Adapted to Survive: Animals That Climb.* Chicago: Heinemann-Raintree, 2014.

Rustad, Martha E. H. *Elephants Are Awesome!* North Mankato, MN: Capstone, 2015.